# WINTERMOON

OTHER WORKS BY ROBERT MACLEAN

BOOKS

*Poems to Define the Corona of Silence* (Fiddlehead, 1970)
*Mantle* (Fiddlehead, 1971)
*Snowglobe* (Fiddlehead, 1973)
*Selected Poems* (Outland Press, 1977)
*In a Canvas Tent* (Sono Nis, 1984)
*Waking to Snow* (Isobar Press, 2020)

CHAPBOOKS

*Heartwood* (Finn Hill Arts, 1986)
*among what is lost* (Cowan & Tetley, 1988)

# WINTERMOON

*Robert MacLean*

ISOBAR
PRESS

First published in 2022 by

Isobar Press
Sakura 2-21-23-202, Setagaya-ku,
Tokyo 156-0053, Japan

&

14 Isokon Flats, Lawn Road,
London NW3 2XD, United Kingdom

https://isobarpress.com

ISBN 978-4-907359-39-3

ACKNOWLEDGEMENTS

A few of these poems have appeared, often in alternative versions, either online or in print in *Kyoto Journal, NOON: journal of the short poem,* and *Ritsumeikan Daigaku Seisaku Kagaku*; and in the small Hailstones anthologies, *Enhaiklopedia, Hailstones: a haiku chapbook, Lost Heian,* and *I Wish.* The haiku 'shaking shuffling' appeared in *The Awakened One: An Anthology,* ed. Adjei Agyei-Baah and Gabriel Rosenstock (Poetry Chaikhana, 2021).

COVER IMAGE
'Tsuki' (Moon) © Sarah Brayer: sarahbrayer.com

for my daughter, Akane

*dusk & dawn*

# Contents

*kangetsu ya    koishi no sawaru    kutsu no soko*

winter moon    pebbles    beneath my shoe

Yosa Buson (1716–84)

## Zazen at Tōfukuji

inbreath at the tip of my nostrils cool
outbreath warm

all day learning
canticles of mist
in the ancient cedars

pulse in the crèche of my wrists
tapped by a miner
trapped underground


Bodhidharma your green eyelids
taste bitter
still I nod off

stare lidlessly
at the floor
until a hole's burned through


fall inside yourself
until that word too
is gone

dawn    the lines in my palm
a few stars deepen

## A Walk by the Kamo River

watching the gray heron
watching
the waterfall

slow rain
breath
of a sleeping child

blind earthworms
drown in puddles
singing




a flock of buds
migrates through the meridian
April

mist tasseling
blue hills
names I don't know




earth after rain
old books
never read

snake crushed on the road
each day smaller
blending in


snail scrawl
on wet
pebbles

cockroach scuttles
across the sidewalk
afraid

where the hermit lived 300 years ago
in the bamboo grove
still a space

cloud floes floating north
why not follow
just throw self away



sun's free fall
arc
to the horizon

even the next door
dog stops
barking


a spider peers
from the rafters
spinning its constellation

creaturely world
translations
from a lost original

## Three-Mat Room

waking
bitterherb
taste of dreams

5 a.m.
old ladies gossiping
by blue garbage bags

cup
shines through
my hand


how to navigate
crowds
deadman's float

suit and necktie
through
the university gates

my voice
a rusty knife
whittling these shavings

even though they seemed
to be listening
how quickly everyone leaves

erase the whiteboard
turn off the light
bow to the empty room

stopping on Kitaoji bridge
look down
my drowned face

surf whisper
in ragged bamboo
outside the shoji

cup of tea
cools
in my hand


trying to sit
zazen
driftwood samadhi

take your heart
down from the shelf
is it beating



blow out the candle
dark
gazes back

if you get lost
far enough
is that home

# Summer Solstice

too hot
for a blanket
midsummer rain

rice paddies
two skies
facing each other


the old workman
dozes
sitting up

packed tight
on hillsides
the dead




light pulses
in the ventricles
of a stone

journey
from nowhere
to nowhere


wind bell
icicles
my distant country

by my buckwheat pillow
cognac amber
Tsukiko's eyes




bees hum
inside
her purr

open window
evening
Heian deep




out there
my home
indigo rain

# Back Route on Fushimi Inari

main path
that way
go this way

bamboo deep-
kissed by rain
aquamarine


salamander
under a log
eyes topaz moons

water glistens
in a snail's
empty shell


language lessons
with a stone
its name its silence

where can
I go where
I'm not


pale *jizō*
face eroded by rain
tipping over

leaf leavening
silence
on the ridge




monarch butterfly
tattered wings
both of us resting

a bird singing
deepens
the mountain

wet stones
shining
first words

returning
feet braille-read the path
in the dark

# Migrations

yardwork
earth in my hand
weighs more than me

ache of the horizon
Kumogahata mountains fragrant
with distance




unshaven all week
in the mirror
my father's face

*I think I'll stay here the service is so good*
cracking jokes
with the ER nurses

my mother could only sip water
from a teaspoon
her last few days

I flew back just in time
to fall asleep
by her bed

opening her eyes
*you must be tired*
then slipped away

my father's tools
hang in the shed
feathered with dust

Autumn


the wind sleepwalks
out of the hills
October


crickets pulse all night
harmonic
of a deeper tuning

the old woman bends
ties rice into sheaves
hands tracing ghosts




frailer each autumn
the old man still hoes his patch
surrounded by high-rises

far off
the ancient voices of children
playing in the park




do cats
listen
to stones

pore over
leaf litter
the colour of lost syllables




caterpillars sleep
on bark
dreaming their cocoons

red dragonflies fuse mid-air
fierce embrace
was I ever so loved



*onna gokoro to aki no sora*
I ask a grad student what it means
her face shifts

black silk rustles
someone undressing
rain

typhoon on the way
salt from the Okinawa islands
on your skin

I put my hand in the icy water
*take back my name*
my fingers whisper



moon's burgeoning belly
midwife stars
gather round

what you were singing all along
cricket
first frost

# Rohatsu *Sesshin* at Tōfukuji

no eyes no ears no tongue
only breath

above the tree-
line
Kyoto's neon

why wait to die
to be still
die while still here

inside the zendo
the only warmth
a stick of incense


*kinhin* in flipflops
rocks float
on snow

too cold
to be cold
the bronze bell vibrates

udon gulped
at breakneck speed
still sitting

400 years
floorboards swirl
the same *makyō*

knees on fire
solar wind
winnows bones

shaking shuffling
Rōshi's last koan
Parkinson's


stepping stones
leading to
a waterfall

train whistle
in the ice blue woods
childhood




hold hand-
lessness
on your lap

snow
before I was born
a roof which breathes



evening star
hummingbird heart

*Oshōgatsu*

Kyoto silent now no traffic
temple bell rings 108 sins
backward to zero

you sip the tea and
look up
your grandmother's eyes

somewhere
in my ice locked body
wings open and close

the bole
dreams
the bark


snow wreathing
city of blue-
tiled roofs

ice glint wintermoon
a few words warmed
by breath



be with me
lady of the nouveau
beaujolais eyes

Pleiades above
the pines
those snowy sisters

# January

the first place we phoned
said he was too small
for ashes

steadfast traveler
journeying inward
the speed of light




lum
inous empti
ness

the blind day
follows
the seeing eye moon

we go to separate rooms
to take off
our faces

nipples still
trickling milk
no one to drink


axe wedge
in my kindling
heart

breath whorl window
snowflakes holding each other
as they fall

# A Meadow in Kibune

between two heartbeats
sit until
your footsteps return

mountains drifting
deep in granite
dream

*once-only*
sings winter wren
again

summer puffballs
luff along
archipelagoes of leaves

am I light
enough
to follow

# Glossary & Notes

# Glossary & Notes

'Bodhidharma your green eyelids': Bodhidharma is the legendary First Patriarch of Chan, who transmitted the Dharma from India to China in the sixth century CE. Often depicted with huge eyes, pupils focused high. The story goes he gazed at the wall of a cave so intensely for nine years that his eyelids fell off (or he sliced them off, to avoid falling asleep); these became the first leaves of the green tea that Zen monks drink to help stay awake.

'dawn        the lines in my palm': the traditional time to end the first pre-dawn zazen, when the lines in one's enfolded hands become visible.

## A WALK BY THE KAMO RIVER

'blind earthworms': a Japanese folk tradition holds that earthworms can sing (*mimizu naku*). Kobayashi Issa (1763–1827) wrote about it several times, as in this haiku translated by Meredith McKinney:

*furuinu ya mimizu no uta ni kanji-gao*

> old dog
> looks like he's sensing
> earthworms' song

## THREE-MAT ROOM

Rooms in Japan are measured by their size in tatami mats (woven rush grass around a rice straw core). Three-mat is fifty square feet, cheap student size.

'Heian deep': the historical period in Japan from 794–1185, in which much of the traditional culture is rooted.

## BACK ROUTE ON FUSHIMI INARI

*jizō*: statue (often carved stone, with a red bib around its neck) of the Bodhissatva Kshitigarbha (earth storehouse/womb), ubiquitous throughout Japan. Originally a guardian of travelers and children, but associated with abortions since the 1960s.

## AUTUMN

*onna gokoro to aki no sora:* a Japanese proverb, 'A woman's heart is like the autumn sky'. For years I thought the vehicle of this trope means the deep beauty of the autumnal sky, until a grad student informed me that it signifies mutability – the constant presence of typhoons in this season: a woman's volatile heart.

## ROHATSU *SESSHIN* AT TŌFUKUJI

A *sesshin* is an intensive training retreat, usually for seven days; literally, 'to gather the mind'. The Rohatsu *sesshin* is held in December to commemorate the Buddha's enlightenment and is noted for its severity.

*kinhin*: walking meditation; *makyō*: hallucinations, usually optical and fragmentary. Literally, 'a devil's condition'. Typically occur around the third or fourth day of the *sesshin*. Usual advice is to ignore them.

For Keidō Fukushima Rōshi (1933–2011).

OSHŌGATSU

On *Oshōgatsu*, New Year's Eve, throughout Japan, temple bells are struck 108 times, voicing the 'snares and delusions' (*bonno*) of tradition. No one today seems quite sure what these 108 sins are, but it's fun trying to find out.

JANUARY

'steadfast traveler': see Robert MacLean, 'Hans Christian Andersen's "The Steadfast Tin Soldier": Variations upon Silence and Love', www.ritsumei.ac.jp/acd/cg/lt/rb/586pdf/maclean.pdf

For Poppy, 10 January 2012, 27 weeks, four days.